LOOK HOW FAR YOU'VE COME

Acknowledging the Distance Traveled in Your Journey

Zera Schmidt

Dedicated to every resilient soul on the journey of self-discovery and personal growth. May this book be a companion in celebrating your progress, navigating challenges with strength, and embracing the incredible individual you've become. Here's to honoring the unique tapestry of your journey and finding inspiration within its pages.

"Perhaps the biggest mistake I made in the past was that I believed love was about finding the right person. In reality, love is about becoming the right person."

In these words, we find the essence of our journey—a recognition that personal growth is an evolution, a continuous transformation into the person we are meant to become. May these words resonate as you navigate the pages of "Look How Far You've Come."

NEIL STRAUSS

"Every morning brings new potential, but only if you embrace it with a willing heart. So open your arms and cherish the opportunity to start afresh."

As the sun rises on each chapter of your life, let these words be a reminder that every moment carries the promise of renewal and growth. May "Look How Far You've Come" be your companion in embracing the potential of each new day on your journey.

ZERA SCHMIDT

CONTENTS

LOOK HOW FAR YOU'VE COME

Acknowledging the Distance
Traveled in Your Journey

Part I

Dear Reader,

Embark on a journey within the pages of "Look How Far You've Come," a celebration of personal growth and a tribute to your unique path of self-discovery. As you hold this book in your hands, let it be a moment of reflection, a pause in the hustle of life, to appreciate the remarkable distance you've traveled since you first stepped onto the path of self-improvement.

The power of reflection often takes a backseat to the relentless pursuit of future aspirations. Yet, within the tales and insights woven into this book, you'll discover the transformative potential of looking back. Take a moment to cast your mind to the beginning of your journey. How have you evolved? What lessons have you learned? "Look How Far

You've Come" is your companion in acknowledging your growth, embracing the challenges you've overcome, and honoring the person you've become.

In a world that clamors for constant progress, the art of reflection is a beacon guiding us to appreciate our achievements, glean wisdom from our experiences, and make purposeful choices for the future. I, too, have faced doubts and felt stuck in my personal growth journey. Yet, through reflection and perseverance, I emerged stronger, realizing the profound importance of embracing my past to recognize my growth.

This book serves as a gentle reminder to resist the whirlwind of daily life, encouraging you to pause, turn inward, and marvel at the progress made on your unique journey. Beyond the pursuit of future goals, "Look How Far You've Come" urges you to appreciate the magnitude of your achievements, offering a moment of stillness in the rush of life.

Obstacles and setbacks are inevitable on the road to personal growth. This book acknowledges these challenges and advocates for resilience and a growth mindset as tools to navigate the peaks and valleys of your journey. It's not about dwelling on the past or fixating on a former self; it's a celebration of your growth—a testament to your resilience, determination, and unwavering spirit.

Within these pages, you'll encounter stories of triumph, tales of perseverance, and moments of self-discovery from kindred spirits who have walked similar paths. Their narratives offer insight into the transformative power of embracing your past, recognizing your growth, and finding inspiration in your journey.

Remember, personal growth is not a linear path but a tapestry of twists, turns, peaks, and valleys. Doubt and uncertainty may arise, but so will moments of immense joy and fulfillment. "Look How Far You've Come" invites you to embrace every facet of this journey, for each experience—setback or success—plays a pivotal role in shaping the person you are today.

Dear reader, let this book be a testament to your remarkable journey. With each turned page, celebrate your progress, acknowledge conquered challenges, and honor the resilient individual you've become. May you find inspiration, motivation, and a profound sense of gratitude for the extraordinary distance you have traveled.

Happy reading, and here's to recognizing and celebrating your journey!

Warm regards.

PREFACE

In the tapestry of life, each of us weaves a unique story- a narrative of growth, resilience, and self-discovery. "Look How Far You've Come" is an exploration of these threads, a collection of narratives and insights designed to resonate with the universal human experience.

As the architect of this journey, I've endeavored to create a space where reflection takes center stage. In a world that often urges us to look ahead, this book encourages you to pause, turn inward, and appreciate the transformative power of introspection.

The pages that follow are not a roadmap but a mosaic of stories, each a testament to the triumphs and tribulations that shape our evolution. From doubt to determination, from setbacks to successes, these tales echo the shared rhythms of the human spirit.

This book is an ode to the seekerâ€"the one on the quest for personal growth, the individual navigating the labyrinth of life. It acknowledges the importance of looking back, not with regret, but with a deep understanding of the lessons learned and the strength gained.

"Look How Far You've Come" is an invitation to celebrate the journey, to acknowledge the progress made, and to honor the person you've become. It is my hope that within these pages, you find resonance, inspiration, and a renewed appreciation for the remarkable distance you've traveled.

So, embark on this literary voyage with an open heart. May these narratives serve as companions, guiding you through the landscape of your own growth and reminding you that, indeed, you have come a long way.

With gratitude and anticipation,

Zera Schmidt

CHAPTER 1

Reflecting on the Past

Introduction

In the hustle and bustle of our daily lives, it's easy to overlook the significance of our past experiences. We often find ourselves looking ahead, chasing new goals and aspirations, without taking the time to pause and reflect on the journey that brought us to this point. However, in this chapter, we will embark on a meaningful exploration of the milestones and significant moments that have shaped your life. Through the power of reflection, we will uncover the transformative power of your past and celebrate how far you've come.

The Power Of Reflection

Reflecting on the past is not simply a nostalgic exercise; it is an essential tool for personal growth and self-awareness. As the renowned psychologist Carl Rogers once said, "The curious paradox is that when

I accept myself just as I am, then I can change" (Rogers, 1961, p. 23).

By delving into the memories and experiences that have shaped your life, you gain a deeper understanding of who you are and the progress you've made. It is through reflection that you can celebrate your achievements, learn from your mistakes, and find inspiration for the future.

In today's fast-paced world, it is easy to get caught up in the constant striving for more—more success, more possessions, more recognition. However, true personal growth lies not only in the pursuit of future goals but also in taking a moment to look back and acknowledge the distance you have traveled. Psychologist Jean Piaget highlighted the importance of reflection when he stated, "Intelligence is what you use when you don't know what to do" (Piaget, 1952, p. 112). In other words, reflection allows us to tap into our inner wisdom, to learn from our past choices, and to gain insight into the person we have become.

Throughout the chapters of this book, you will encounter stories and insights from notable authors and researchers who have studied the power of reflection and its impact on personal growth. Psychologist Daniel Kahneman, in his book "Thinking, Fast, and Slow," explores the concept of introspection and how it influences decision-making (Kahneman, 2011). By understanding our own biases and reflecting on our thought processes, we can make more informed choices and navigate the complexities of life with greater clarity.

Another influential figure in the realm of reflection and self-awareness is Dr. Brené Brown, a research professor and storyteller. In her book "The Gifts of Imperfection," she emphasizes the importance of embracing vulnerability and allowing ourselves to be seen as we truly are (Brown, 2010). Through reflection, we can uncover our authentic selves, recognize our strengths, and cultivate a sense of compassion for our journey.

As you embark on this exploration of reflection and personal growth, remember that it is a journey unique to you. There is no right or wrong way to reflect, and the process may look different for each individual. Some may find solace in journaling, while others may seek guidance through meditation or engaging in meaningful conversations. Whatever method resonates with you, make a commitment to set aside dedicated time for introspection and self-discovery.

In the pages that follow, we will delve into the transformative power of reflection. We will explore how celebrating your achievements, learning from your mistakes, and finding inspiration for the future are integral to your personal growth. Each story and insight shared within these chapters will serve as a gentle nudge to look inward, to embrace the lessons of your past, and to celebrate the incredible journey of growth that has brought you to this point.

So, dear reader, let us embark on this voyage together. Let us delve into the depths of our experiences, uncover our true selves, and celebrate the progress we have made. Through reflection, we can stand in awe of how far we have come, and with that knowledge, we can confidently move forward into the boundless possibilities that lie ahead.

Exploring Milestones

Throughout our lives, we encounter significant milestones that mark pivotal moments of growth and change. These milestones can be personal, professional, or even spiritual in nature. They have the power to shape our identities, alter our perspectives, and propel us forward on our journey of self-discovery. As you hold this book in your hands, I invite you to embark on a journey of reflection and exploration—a journey that will enable you to recognize and appreciate the milestones that have shaped your remarkable path.

The beauty of milestones lies in their diversity. They can take various forms and occur at different stages of our lives. Perhaps it was the day you walked across the stage to receive your diploma, signifying years of hard work and dedication. Or maybe it was the moment you received that long-awaited promotion, validating your skills and opening new doors of opportunity. Milestones can also manifest as transformative journeys, both physical and metaphorical, that expose us to different cultures, perspectives, and ways of being. And let us not forget the profound impact of relationships—a chance encounter, a lifelong friendship, or a romantic partnership that forever alters the course of our lives.

In contemplating your own milestones, I encourage you to immerse yourself fully in the memories associated with each one. Allow yourself to recall the emotions, the challenges, and the triumphs you experienced during those transformative turning points. Acknowledge the lessons learned, the growth achieved, and the strengths uncovered along the way. This process of introspection will not only deepen your understanding of yourself but also provide valuable insights into the person you've become.

As you embark on this exploration, it is important to recognize that the power of milestones extends beyond the individual. Our personal growth and achievements are often influenced by the wisdom and guidance of others. As we delve into the stories of remarkable individuals who have traversed their own journeys of milestones, we will draw inspiration from and learn from their experiences. Through their narratives, we will discover common threads that connect us all, illuminating the universal nature of personal growth and the significance of celebrating our accomplishments.

In "Look How Far You've Come," we will journey alongside renowned authors and experts such as Dr. Angela Duckworth, whose groundbreaking research on grit and perseverance can shed light on the resilience needed to overcome obstacles and reach our milestones. We will also delve into the wisdom of Dr. Carol Dweck, whose work on mindset reveals the transformative power of embracing a growth-oriented perspective as we navigate our milestones. Through their invaluable insights and those of other esteemed contributors, we will gain a deeper understanding of our own journeys and the milestones that have shaped us.

Before we embark on this transformative exploration, it is crucial to remember that personal growth is not a solitary endeavor. It is through shared experiences, shared insights, and shared celebrations that we truly thrive. So, dear reader, let us embark on this journey together, acknowledging the milestones that have defined our paths and celebrating the incredible progress we have made. Through reflection and exploration, we will uncover the wisdom within and honor the unique tapestry of milestones that have brought us to this moment.

Key Authors On Reflection

In the vast realm of personal growth and self-discovery, several authors have shed light on the transformative power of reflection. Through their profound insights and scholarly works, they have offered guidance on how to navigate the labyrinth of our own experiences and uncover the wisdom hidden within. Let us embark on a journey through the wisdom of two key authors who have delved into the essence of reflection: John Dewey and Daniel Kahneman.

John Dewey, a prominent American philosopher and educator, emphasized the vital role of reflection in the process of learning. In his influential book "How We Think" (1933), Dewey expounds on the significance of thoughtful reflection as a means to make sense of our experiences and bridge the gap between abstract theories and practical application. According to Dewey, reflection enables us to engage in active thought by asking probing questions and exploring different perspectives. It is through this deliberate examination of our experiences that we acquire a deeper understanding and extract valuable insights to guide our future actions. As you embark on this journey of reflection, Dewey's work will serve as a guiding light, reminding you of the inherent value of pausing to reflect and consciously engage with your own experiences.

Another luminary in the realm of cognitive psychology and decision-making, Daniel Kahneman, has revolutionized our understanding of human thought processes in his groundbreaking work "Thinking, Fast, and Slow" (2011). Kahneman introduces us to the two systems of thought that govern our decision-making: the fast and intuitive System 1 and the slower, deliberate System 2. He emphasizes that System 2, characterized by reflective and analytical thinking, plays a crucial role in making wise choices and avoiding cognitive biases. Kahneman's research underscores the importance of giving ourselves the space and time for reflection, allowing us to move beyond impulsive reactions and delve deeper into the complexities of our experiences. As you embark on this journey of self-reflection, Kahneman's insights will equip you with the tools to navigate the intricate workings of your mind and make more informed decisions.

In "Look How Far You've Come," we draw upon the wisdom of these distinguished authors and many others to guide you in your personal growth journey. Each chapter is carefully curated to illuminate different facets of reflection, drawing inspiration from research, personal narratives, and practical exercises. By embracing the power of reflection, you will unlock new perspectives, cultivate self-awareness, and harness the transformative potential within you.

Conclusion

In this chapter, we have begun our journey of reflection, recognizing the importance of looking back on our past experiences and milestones. By embracing the transformative power of reflection and drawing insights from key authors, we set the stage for celebrating your personal growth. As we move forward in this book, we will continue to explore the depths of your journey, discovering the lessons learned and the wisdom gained along the way. So, let us now turn the page and delve deeper into the remarkable tapestry of your life.

CHAPTER 2

Recognizing Growth and Achievements

Welcome to Chapter 2 of "Look How Far You've Come." In this chapter, we will explore the significance of recognizing our personal growth and achievements. It is easy to get caught up in the demands and challenges of life, often neglecting to acknowledge our progress. By learning to identify and celebrate our accomplishments, we can boost our self-confidence, enhance our motivation, and foster a positive mindset. Throughout this chapter, we will delve into the importance of acknowledging progress, discuss the benefits of celebrating successes, and provide practical exercises to help you assess your growth.

Recognizing Progress

In the hustle and bustle of our fast-paced society, it's easy to get caught up in the relentless pursuit of our next goal. We set our sights on the horizon, driven by ambition and the desire to achieve more. However, in our relentless pursuit, we often forget to pause and appreciate how far we have come.

Recognizing progress is a vital practice that involves acknowledging the milestones we have achieved, both big and small. It requires us to take a step back, reflect on our journey, and assess the skills we have developed along the way. By recognizing our progress, we not only celebrate our accomplishments but also gain a deeper understanding of our personal growth and development.

Renowned psychologist Carol S. Dweck (2006) emphasizes the significance of recognizing progress in fostering a growth mindset. When we take the time to acknowledge our achievements, we reinforce the belief that our efforts and abilities can lead to success. This reinforcement strengthens our self-belief, boosts our self-confidence, and ultimately motivates us to continue striving for our goals.

Imagine embarking on a challenging project or learning a new skill. Initially, it may feel overwhelming and insurmountable. However, as you invest time and effort, you start to make progress. Maybe you complete a difficult task, acquire new knowledge, or overcome a significant obstacle. These milestones are not to be overlooked or dismissed. They are indicators of growth, evidence that your hard work is paying off.

Recognizing progress is not limited to grand achievements or reaching the finish line. It's about acknowledging the incremental steps and the small victories that pave the way towards our ultimate objectives. Every milestone, no matter how insignificant it may seem, is a testament to your dedication and perseverance.

To cultivate a habit of recognizing progress, take a moment to reflect on your journey. Consider the challenges you have faced, the skills you have developed, and the personal growth you have experienced. Write them down in a journal or share them with a trusted friend or mentor. By documenting your progress, you create a tangible reminder of how far you have come.

As you embark on your journey of self-improvement and personal development, remember that recognizing progress is not a one-time activity. It's an ongoing practice that allows you to appreciate your achievements, build self-confidence, and fuel your motivation. Embrace the mindset of growth, and with each step forward, take a moment to acknowledge and celebrate your progress.

Celebrating Success:

In our journey of personal growth and accomplishment, it is essential to pause and celebrate our successes. Far from being a self-indulgent act, celebrating our achievements is a crucial practice for our psychological well-being. When we take the time to acknowledge and rejoice in our accomplishments, we tap into a wealth of positive emotions that have far-reaching effects on our overall happiness and satisfaction with life.

According to Fredrickson's broaden-and-build theory (2001), positive emotions serve as catalysts for expanding our cognitive and behavioral patterns. When we celebrate our successes, we ignite a cascade of positive emotions such as joy, pride, and gratitude. These emotions not only bring immediate pleasure but also have long-term benefits.

Firstly, celebrating success broadens our thinking. It opens our minds to new possibilities and opportunities. In the midst of celebrating, we become more receptive to alternative perspectives, innovative ideas, and creative solutions. This expanded mindset allows us to approach future challenges with a greater sense of flexibility and adaptability.

Moreover, celebrating our accomplishments enhances our resilience. When we take the time to reflect on the milestones we have reached, we reinforce our belief in our own abilities and strengths. This bolstered self-confidence serves as a valuable resource when facing obstacles or setbacks. It reminds us that we have overcome challenges before and have the capability to do so again. With resilience, we can weather storms and bounce back stronger than ever.

Additionally, celebrating success nurtures our problem-solving abilities. The positive emotions we experience during celebrations sharpen our cognitive functions, enabling us to think more creatively and effectively. This heightened cognitive state empowers us to approach complex situations with a fresh perspective, leading to more innovative solutions and better outcomes.

To fully embrace the practice of celebrating success, take the time to reflect on your achievements, big and small. Consider the goals you have accomplished, the obstacles you have overcome, and the progress you have made. Allow yourself to bask in the joy, pride, and gratitude that arise from these reflections. Share your successes with others, whether it be with friends, family, or mentors, and invite them to join in your celebration. By sharing our accomplishments, we not only amplify the positive emotions within ourselves but also inspire and uplift those around us.

Exercises For Assessing Growth

In order to truly recognize your growth and achievements, it is important to engage in self-reflection and assessment. The following exercises are designed to help you gain a deeper understanding of your progress, strengths, and areas for further development. By actively participating in these exercises, you will be able to celebrate your accomplishments and set a solid foundation for future growth.

Exercise 1: Reflective Journaling

Reflective journaling is a powerful tool for self-discovery and personal growth. Find a quiet and comfortable space where you can reflect without distractions. Take out a journal or open a document on your computer and engage in the following prompts:

1. **Challenges Overcome:** Write about the challenges you have faced throughout your personal and professional journey. Reflect on how you overcame these obstacles, the strategies you employed, and the lessons you learned. Consider the resilience and determination that drove you forward.

2. **Acquired Skills:** Identify the skills you have acquired along the way. These skills can be both technical and interpersonal. Write about how these skills have contributed to your growth and success. Consider

how you have applied them in various situations and the positive impact they have had on your outcomes.

3. Milestones Achieved: List the significant milestones you have achieved in your life. These can be personal, professional, or even educational milestones. Reflect on the effort, dedication, and perseverance it took to reach these milestones. Consider the growth and transformation that occurred during the pursuit of these goals.

4. Shaping Identity: Reflect on how your experiences, challenges, skills, and milestones have shaped your identity. Consider the values, beliefs, and strengths that have emerged from your journey. Write about the person you have become as a result of your growth and achievements.

Exercise 2: Strengths Inventory

Understanding your strengths is vital to recognizing your growth and achievements. This exercise will help you identify and appreciate your unique qualities. Grab a pen and paper or create a new document, and follow these steps:

1. List Your Strengths: Make a comprehensive list of your strengths and talents. These can include qualities such as creativity, resilience, leadership, problem-solving, empathy, or any other positive attributes you possess. Don't be modest—acknowledge and embrace your strengths.

2. Reflect on Utilization: Reflect on how you have utilized these strengths in different areas of your life. Consider situations where you have effectively applied your strengths and achieved positive outcomes. Write about specific examples that highlight the impact your strengths have had on your growth and achievements.

3. Recognize growth: Consider how your strengths have evolved over time. Reflect on how you have developed and refined these qualities. Write about the growth you have experienced in utilizing your strengths and the subsequent positive changes it has brought to your life.

Exercise 3: Feedback Assessment

Seeking feedback from trusted individuals can provide valuable insights into your growth and progress. Here's how you can engage in a feedback assessment:

1. Identify Trusted Individuals: Choose a few individuals in your life who know you well and whose opinions you trust. This can include mentors, friends, colleagues, or family members. Reach out to them and explain that you are seeking their feedback to help assess your growth.

2. Ask for Feedback: Request specific feedback on your personal and professional growth. Ask them to identify areas where they have observed growth in you or positive changes they have noticed. Encourage them to provide constructive feedback that can help you gain a clearer perspective on your achievements.

3. Reflect and Evaluate: Once you have collected feedback from multiple sources, take the time to reflect on their insights. Compare their observations with your own perceptions of progress. Consider the common themes or patterns that emerge. Reflect on how this feedback aligns with your self-assessment and use it as a basis for further growth.

Engaging in exercises that assess your growth is an important step in recognizing your accomplishments. Through reflective journaling, a strengths inventory, and seeking feedback, you gain a deeper understanding of how far you have come and the strengths you possess. These exercises enable you to celebrate your achievements, reinforce a growth mindset, and lay the groundwork for future growth.

By reflecting on your personal and professional journey, acknowledging the challenges you have overcome, and recognizing the skills you have acquired, you develop a sense of self-awareness and appreciation for your growth. Furthermore, identifying and utilizing your strengths helps you leverage them to achieve positive outcomes in various areas of your life.

Additionally, seeking feedback from trusted individuals provides valuable perspectives and insights that can enhance your self-assessment. The feedback you receive helps you gain a clearer picture of your growth and progress, validating your accomplishments and motivating you to continue on your journey of personal and professional development.

As you engage in these exercises, remember to approach them with a growth mindset and an open heart. Embrace the opportunities to celebrate how far you have come and recognize the potential for continued growth. Your accomplishments deserve acknowledgement, and by doing so, you pave the way for even greater achievements in the future.

Conclusion:

Recognizing our growth and achievements is an essential practice for personal and professional development. By taking the time to acknowledge progress and celebrate successes, we enhance our self-confidence, foster a growth mindset, and boost our overall well-being. Through the exercises provided in this chapter, you can assess your growth, identify your strengths, and gain a deeper understanding of your journey thus far.

Remember, you have come a long way, and your accomplishments deserve to be acknowledged and celebrated. In the next chapter, we will explore strategies for setting meaningful goals that align with your values and aspirations. So, keep turning the pages, and let's continue on this journey of self-discovery and growth.

REFERENCES

Dewey, J. (1933). *How We Think*. D.C. Heath and Company.

Dweck, C. S. (2006). *Mindset: The New Psychology of Success*. Random House.

Fredrickson, B. L. (2001). The role of positive emotions in positive psychology: The broaden-and-build theory of positive emotions. *American Psychologist, 56*(3), 218-226.

Brown, B. (2010). *The Gifts of Imperfection: Let Go of Who You Think You're Supposed to Be and Embrace Who You Are*. Hazelden Publishing.

Kahneman, D. (2011). *Thinking, Fast and Slow*. Farrar, Straus and Giroux.

Piaget, J. (1952). *The Origins of Intelligence in Children*. New York: International Universities Press.

Rogers, C. R. (1961). *On Becoming a Person: A Therapist's View of Psychotherapy*. London: Constable.

Additional Recommended Readings:

1. Grant, A. M. (2019). *The Power of Moments: Why Certain Experiences Have Extraordinary Impact*. Simon & Schuster.
2. Seligman, M. E. P. (2006). *Learned Optimism: How to Change Your Mind and Your Life*. Vintage.
3. Sivers, D. (2011). *Anything You Want: 40 Lessons for a New Kind of Entrepreneur*. Portfolio.